ALL RIGHT RESERVED © 2020

NO PART OF THIS PUBLICATION
MAY BE REPRODUCED, DISTRIBUTED
OR TRANSMITTED IN ANY FORM OR BY ANY
MEANS, INCLUDING PHOTOCOPYING,
RECORDING OR OTHER ELECTRONIC OR
MECANICAL METHODS WITHOUT THE PRIOR
WRITTEN PERMISSION OF THE PUBLISHER,
EXCEPT IN THE CASE OF BRIEF QUOTATION
EMBODIED IN CRITICAL REVIEWS AND CERTAIN
OTHER NON COMMERCIAL USES PERMITTED
BY COPYRIGHT LAW

THIS COLORING BOOK BELONGS TO:

ALL RIGHTS RESERVED © 2020

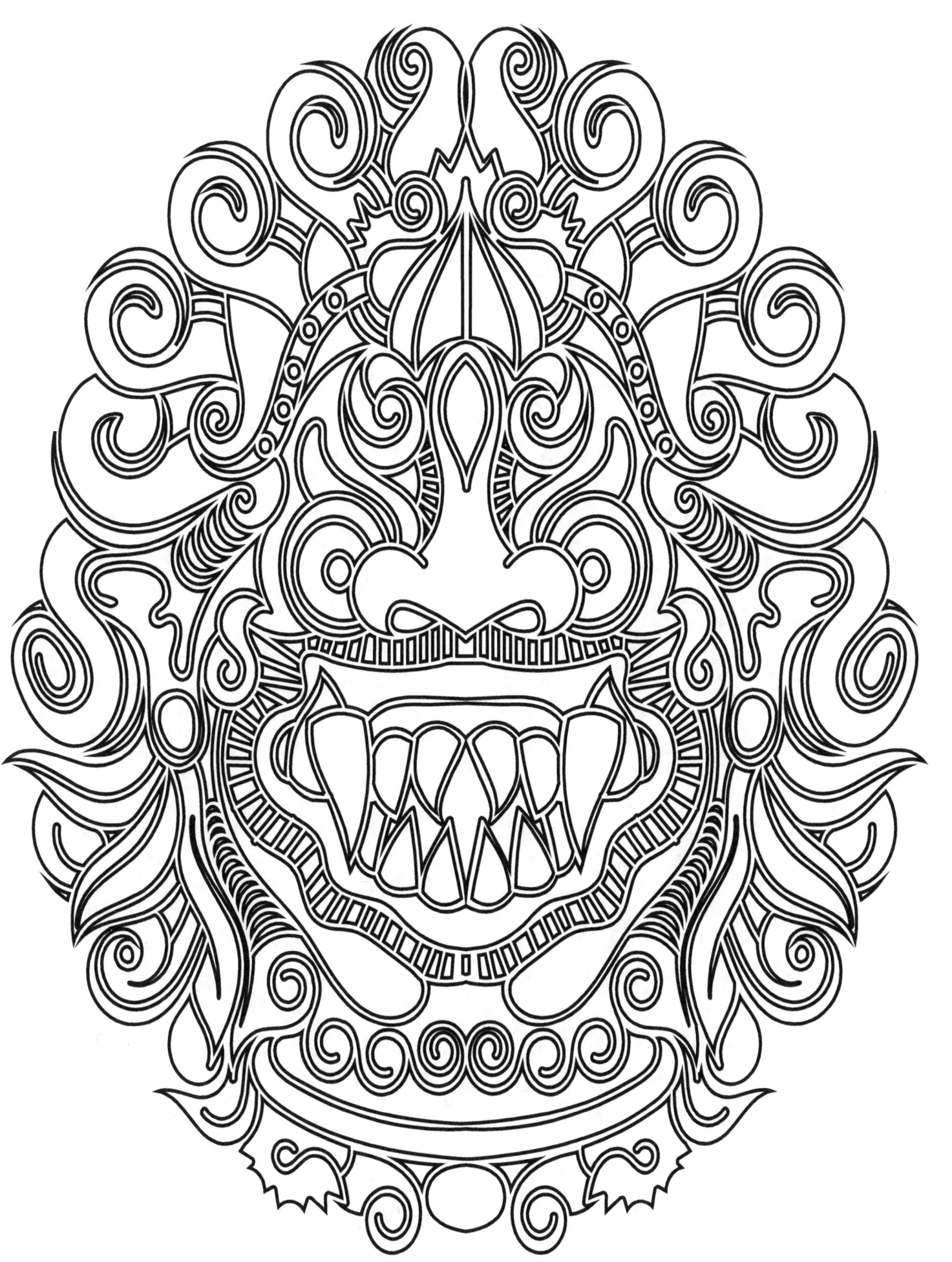

ALL RIGHTS RESERVED © 2020

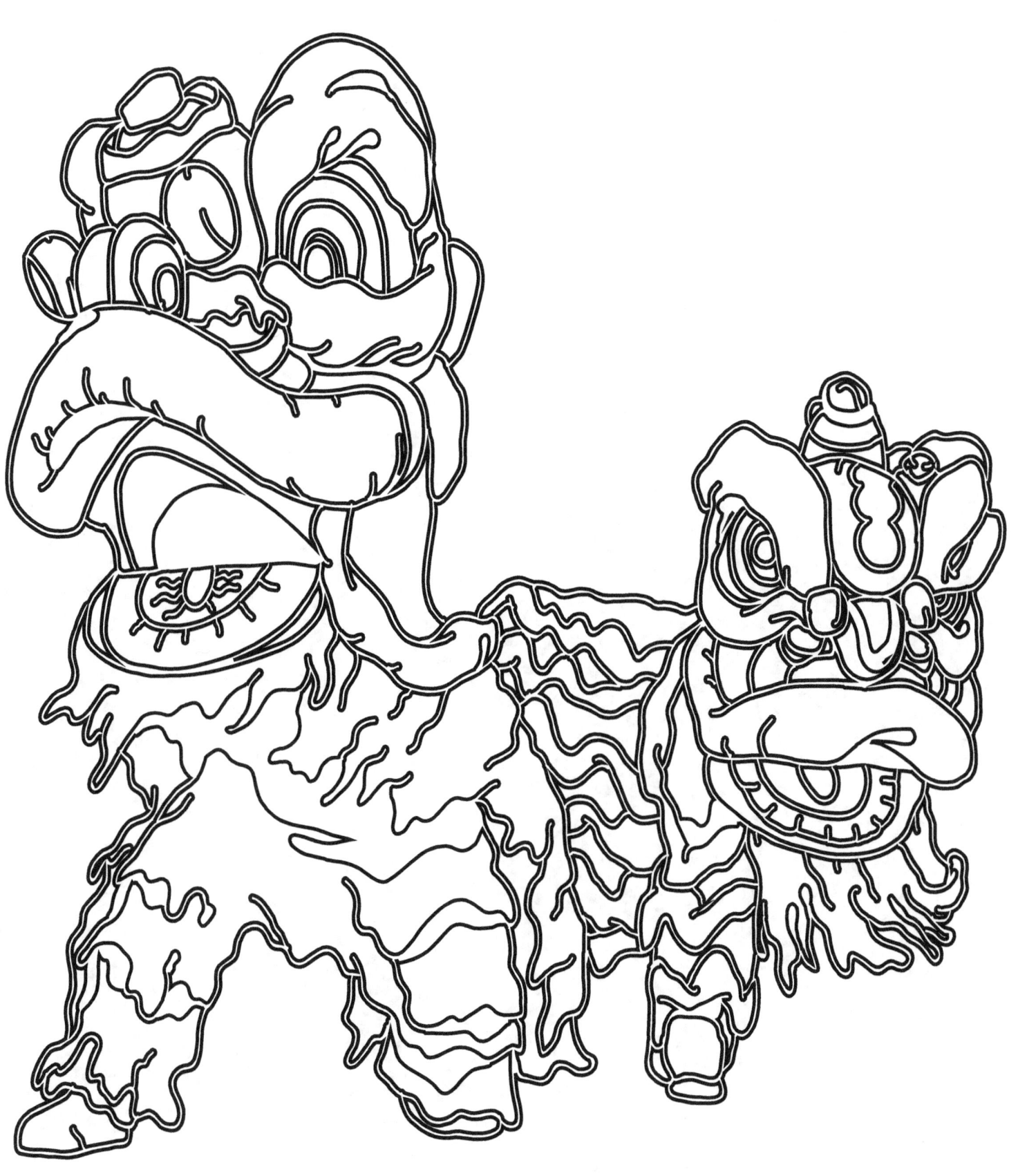

ALL RIGHTS RESERVED © 2020

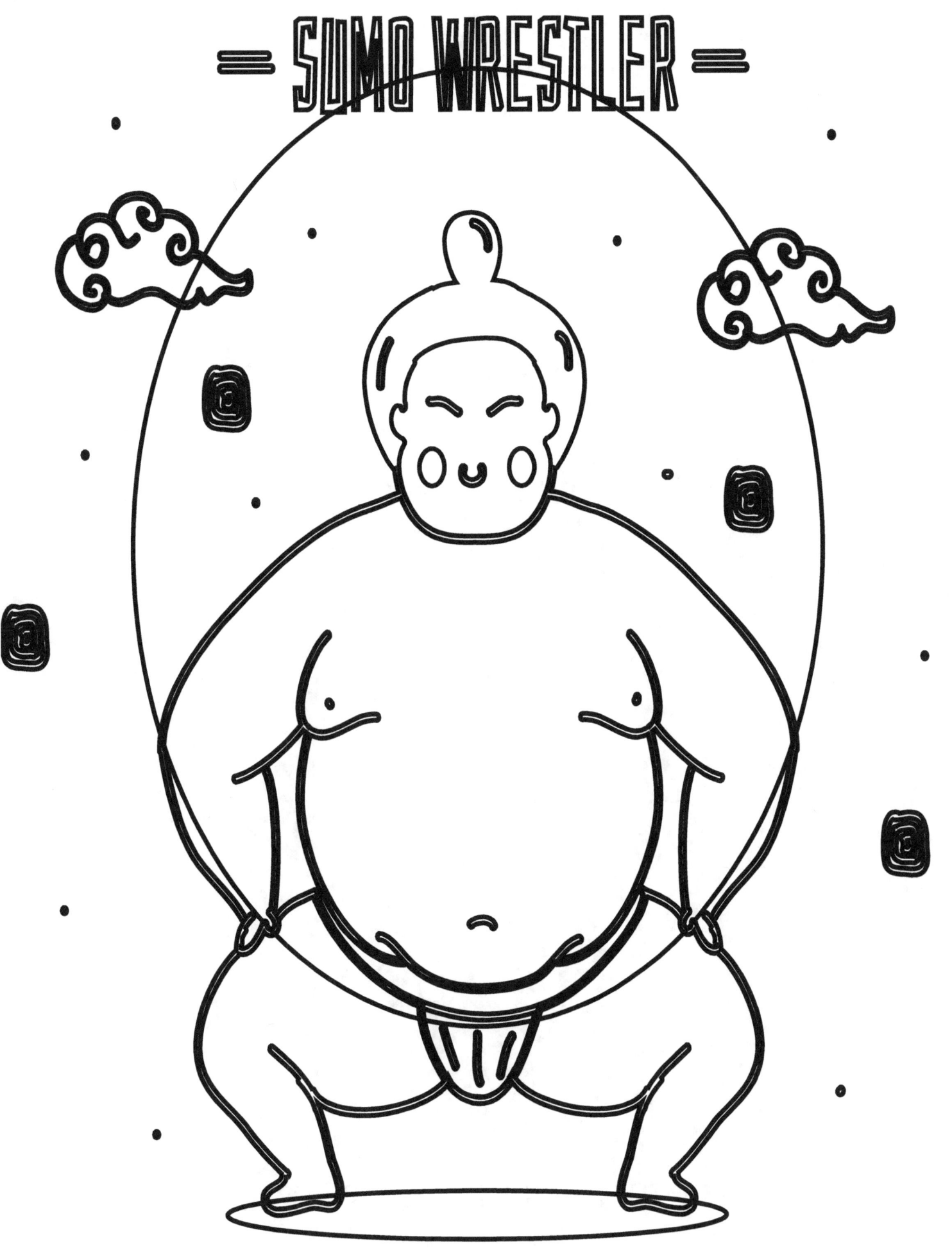

ALL RIGHTS RESERVED © 2020

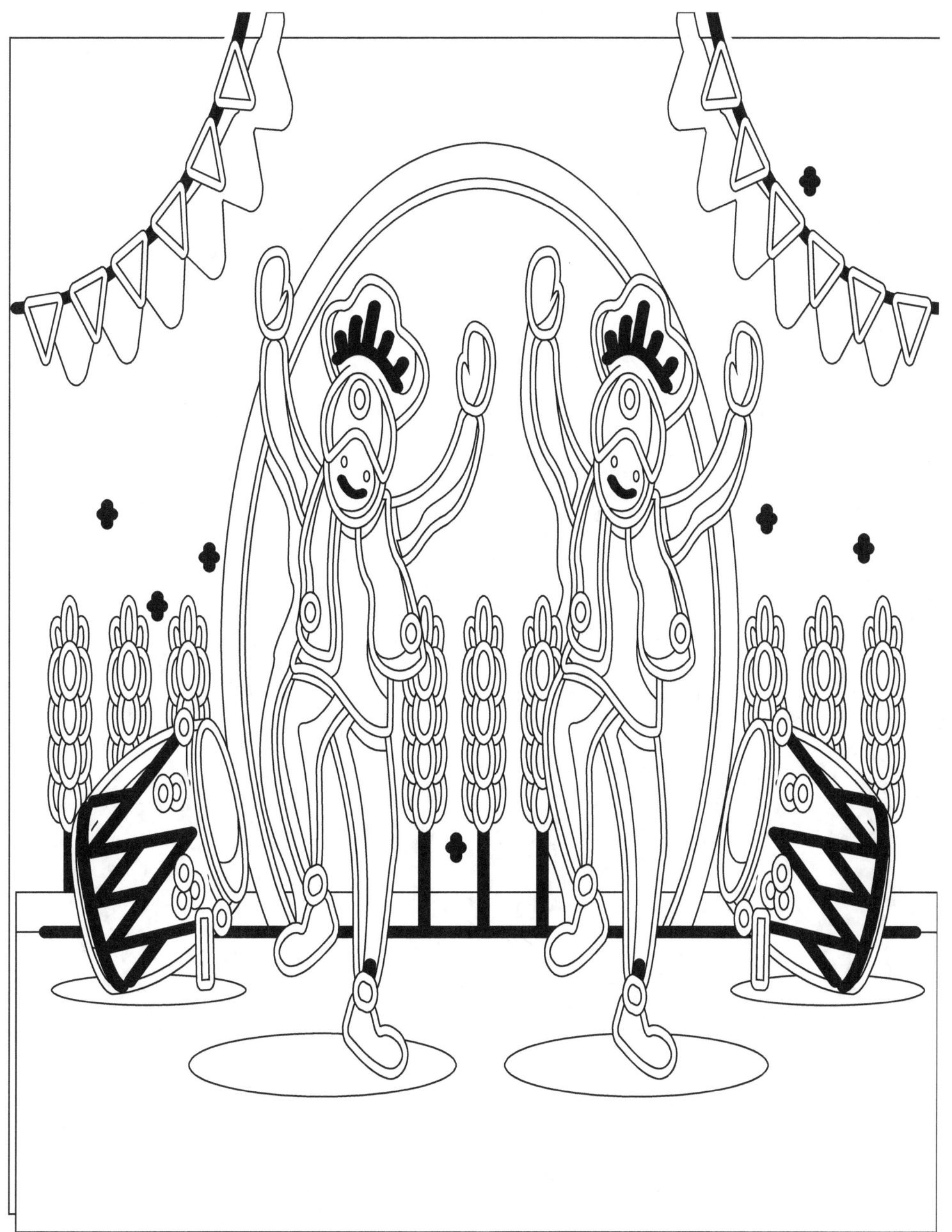

ALL RIGHTS RESERVED © 2020

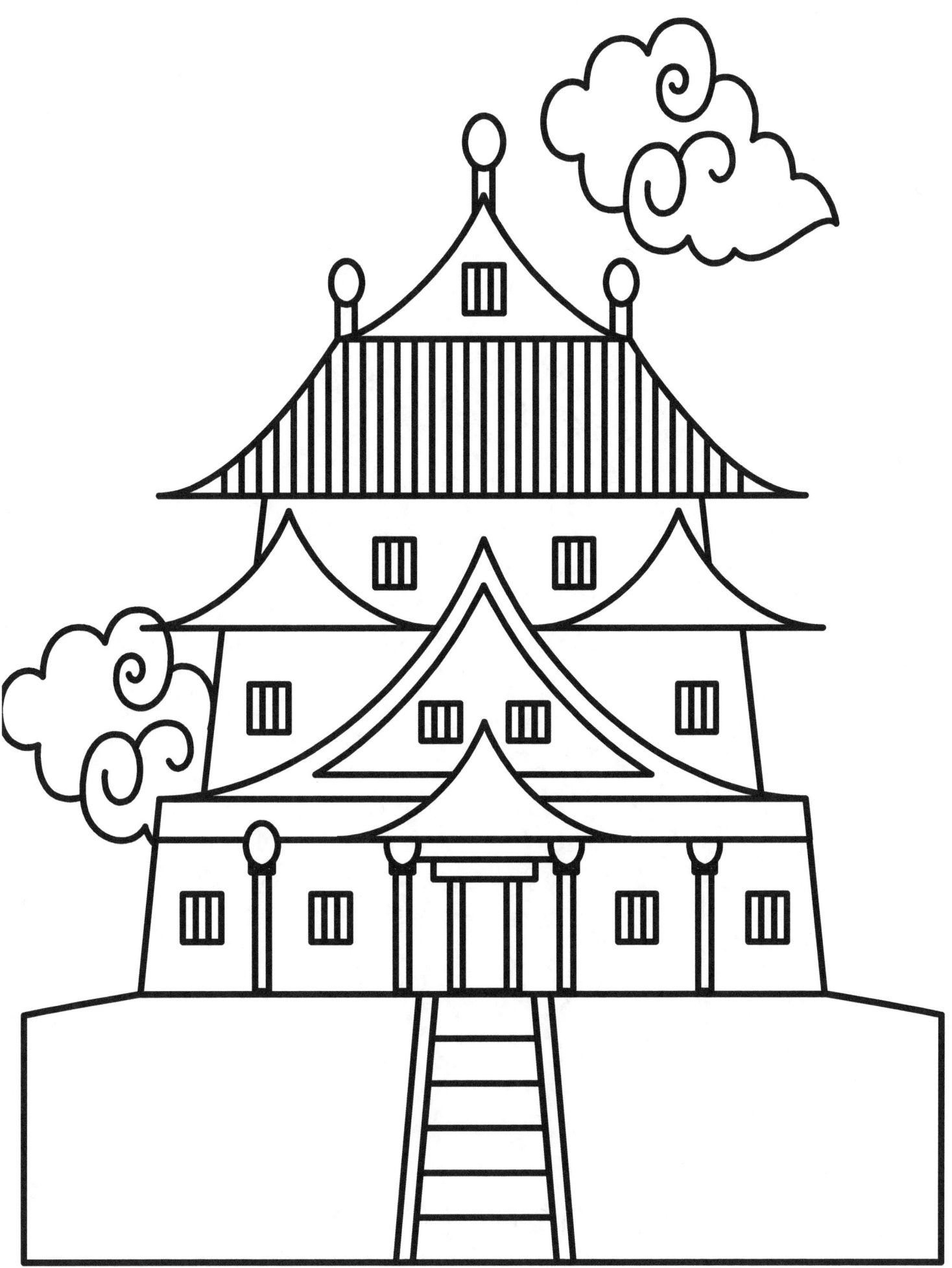

ALL RIGHTS RESERVED © 2020

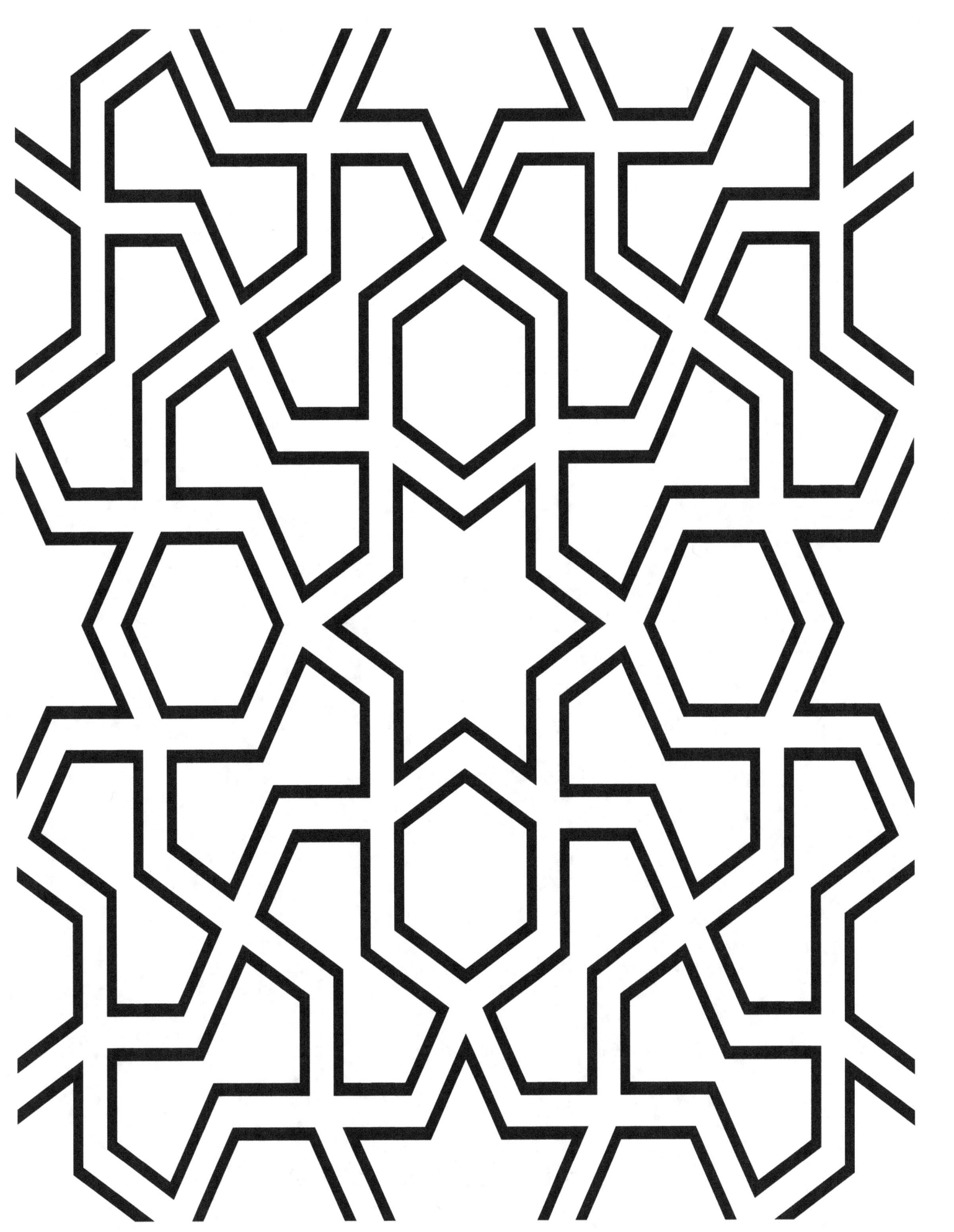

ALL RIGHTS RESERVED © 2020

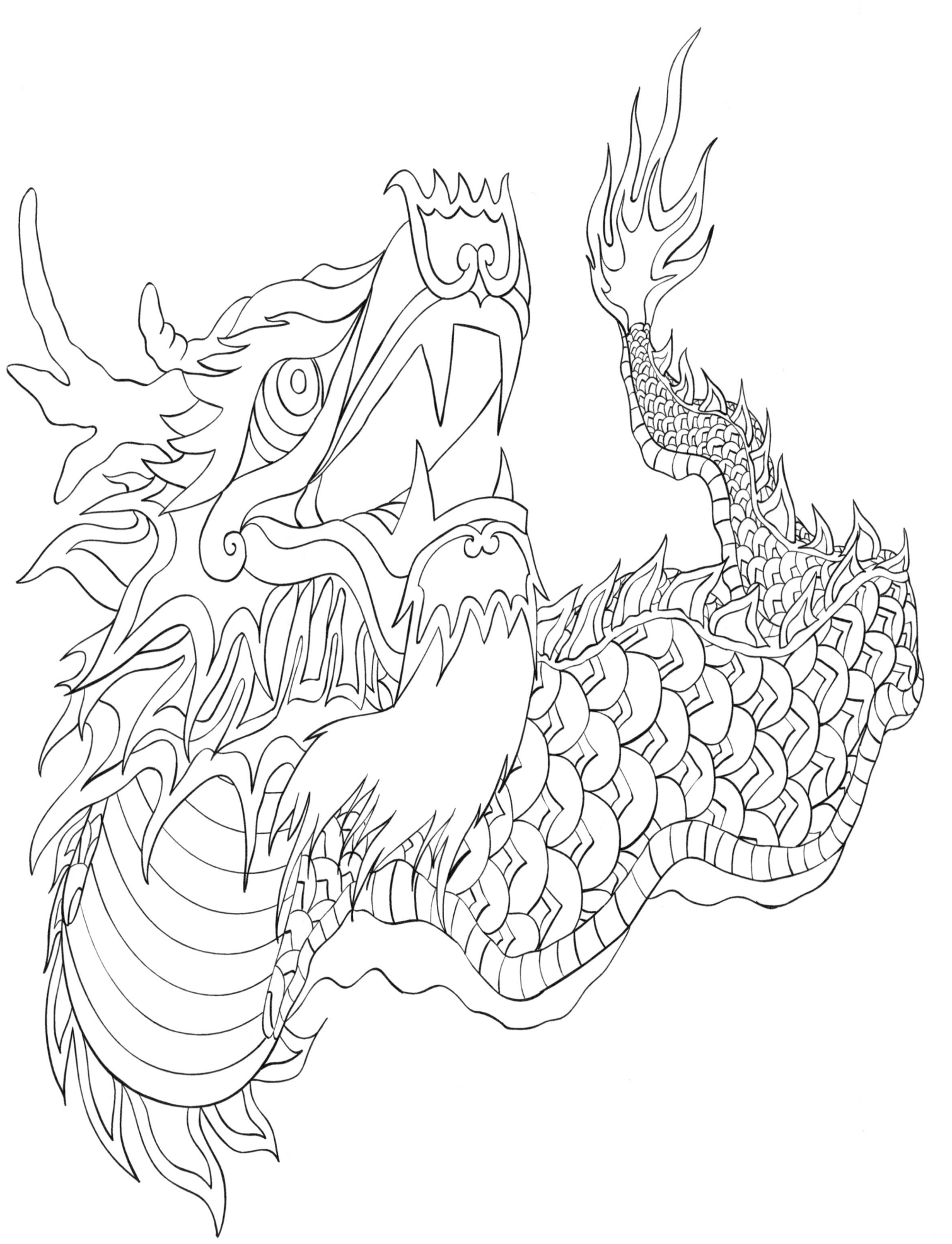

ALL RIGHTS RESERVED © 2020

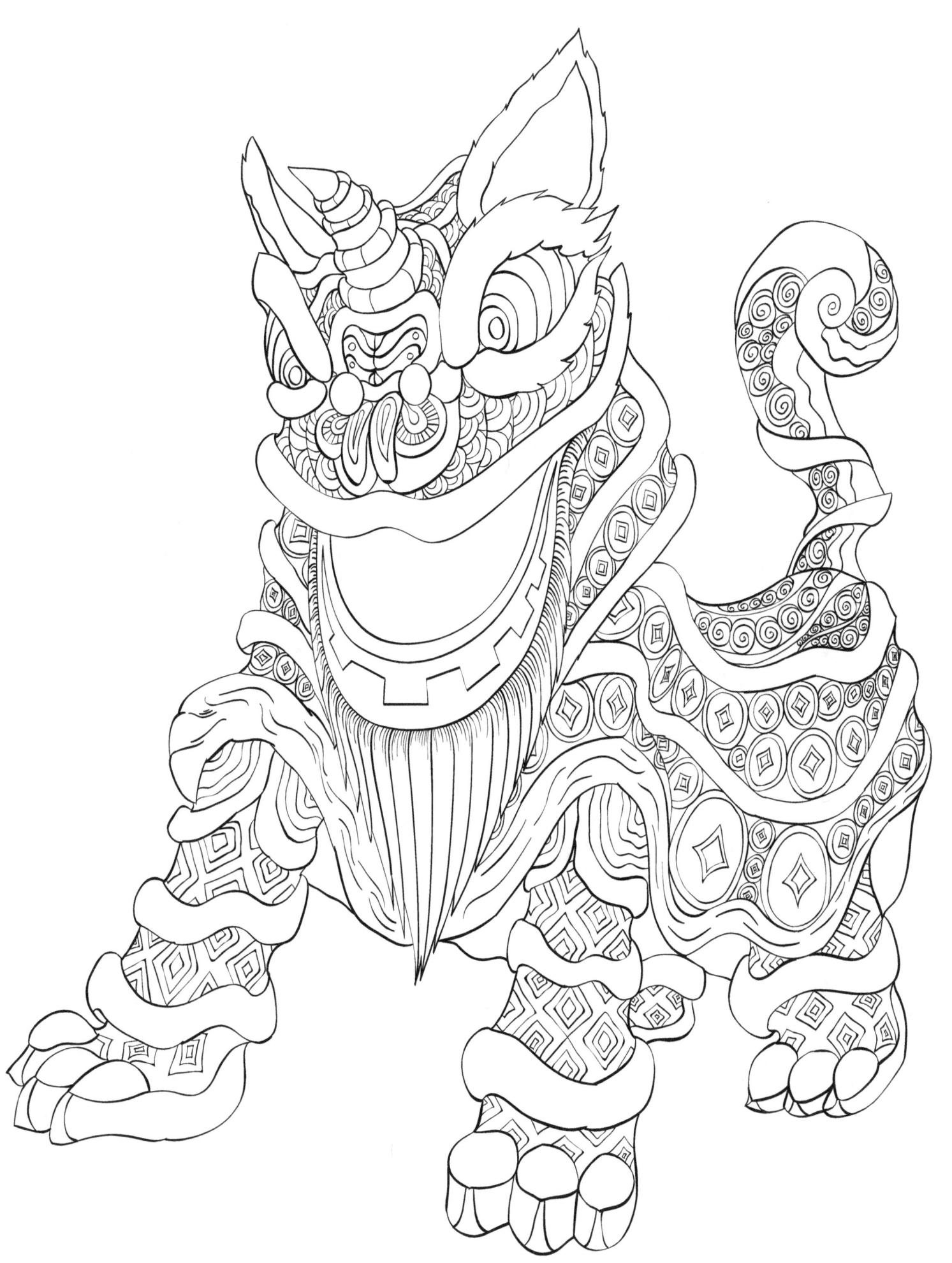

ALL RIGHTS RESERVED © 2020

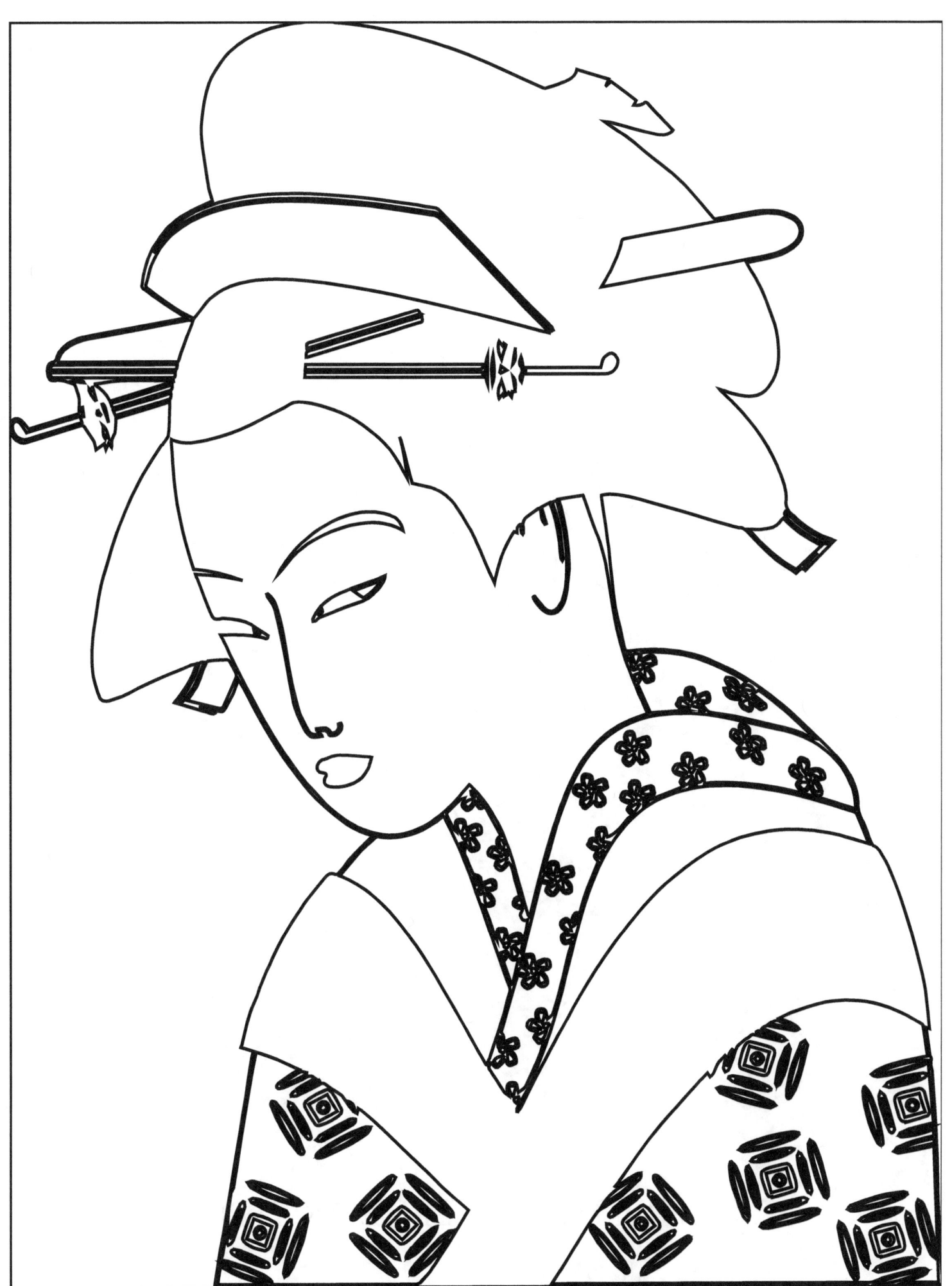

ALL RIGHTS RESERVED © 2020

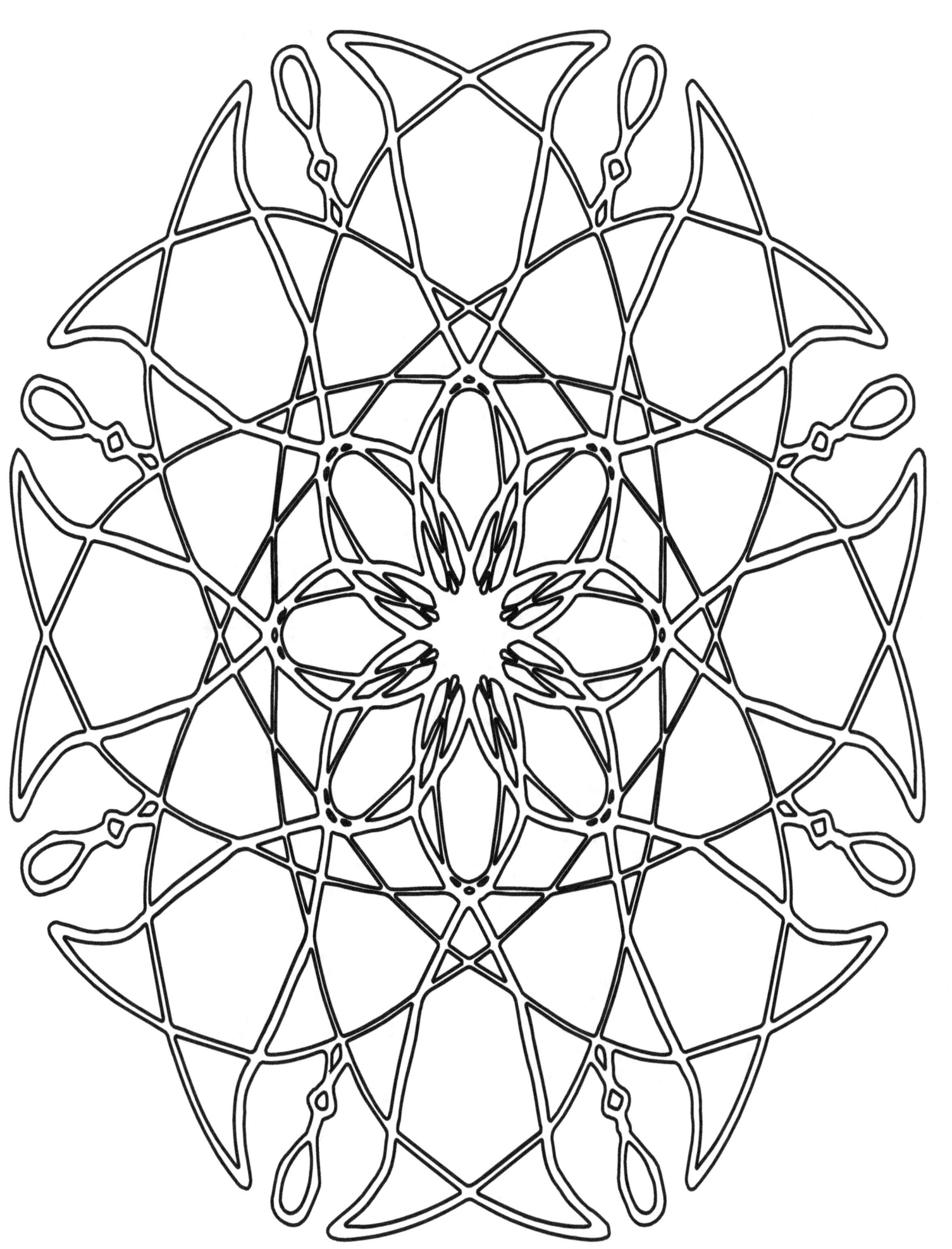

ALL RIGHTS RESERVED © 2020

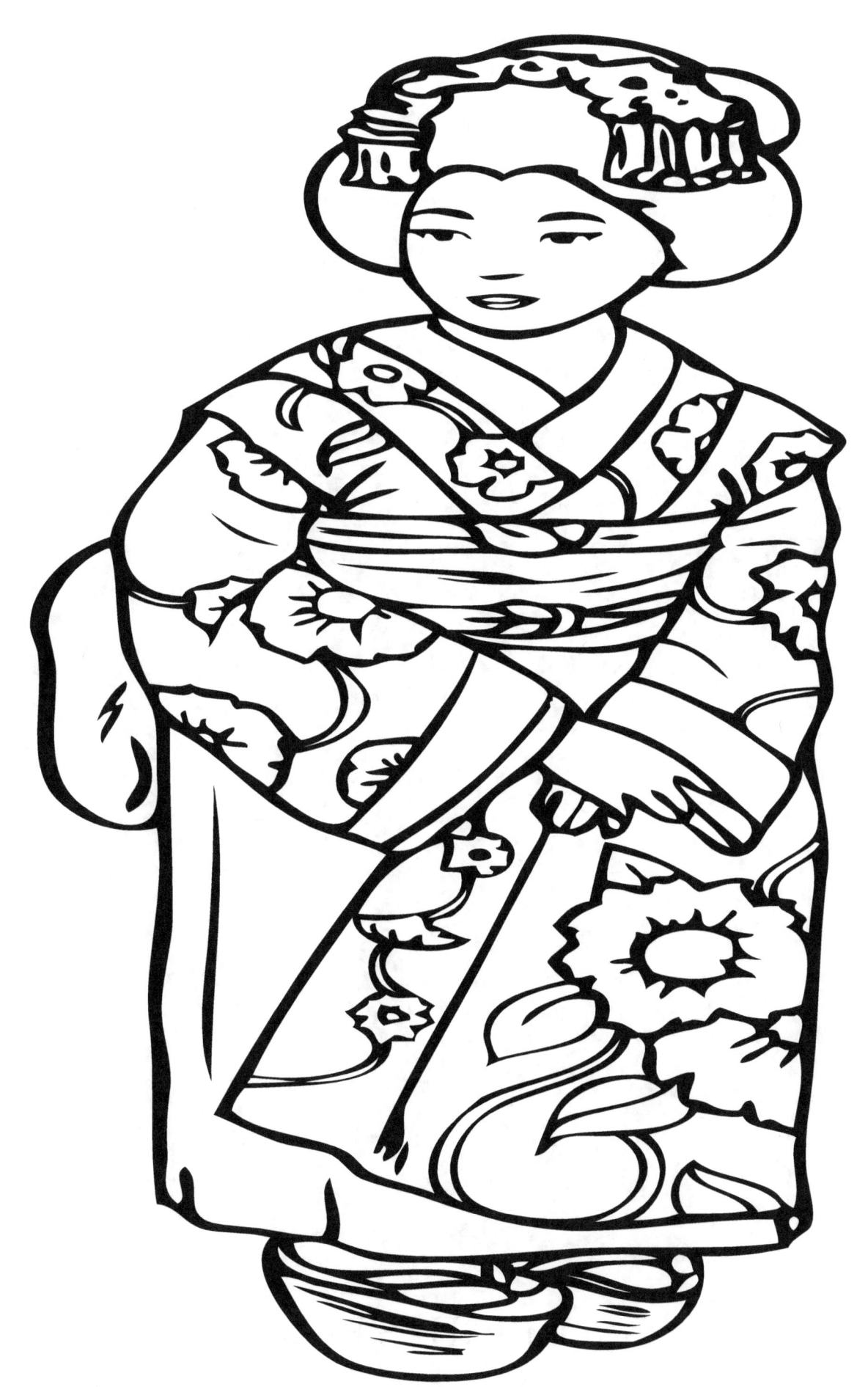

ALL RIGHTS RESERVED © 2020

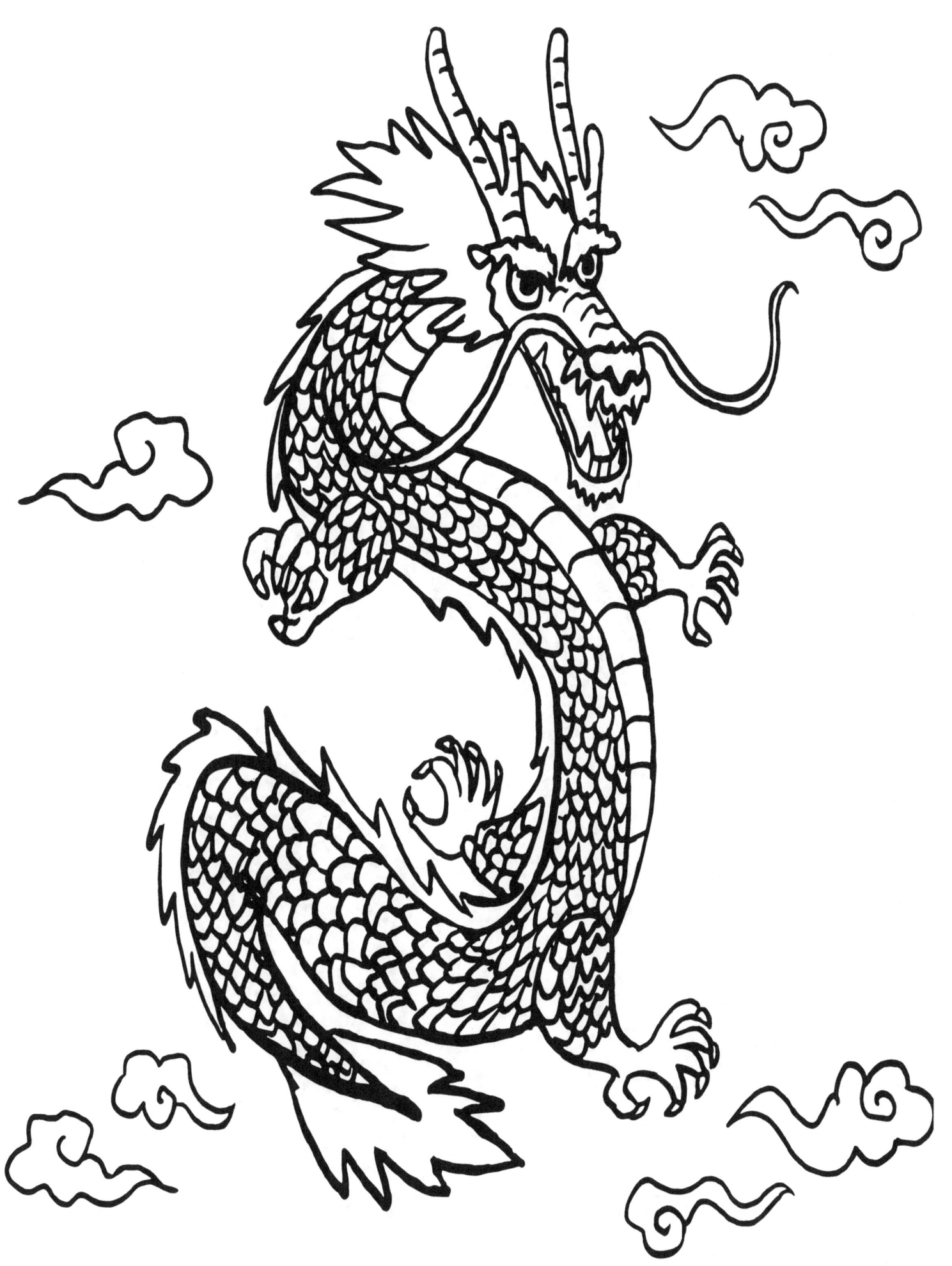

ALL RIGHTS RESERVED © 2020

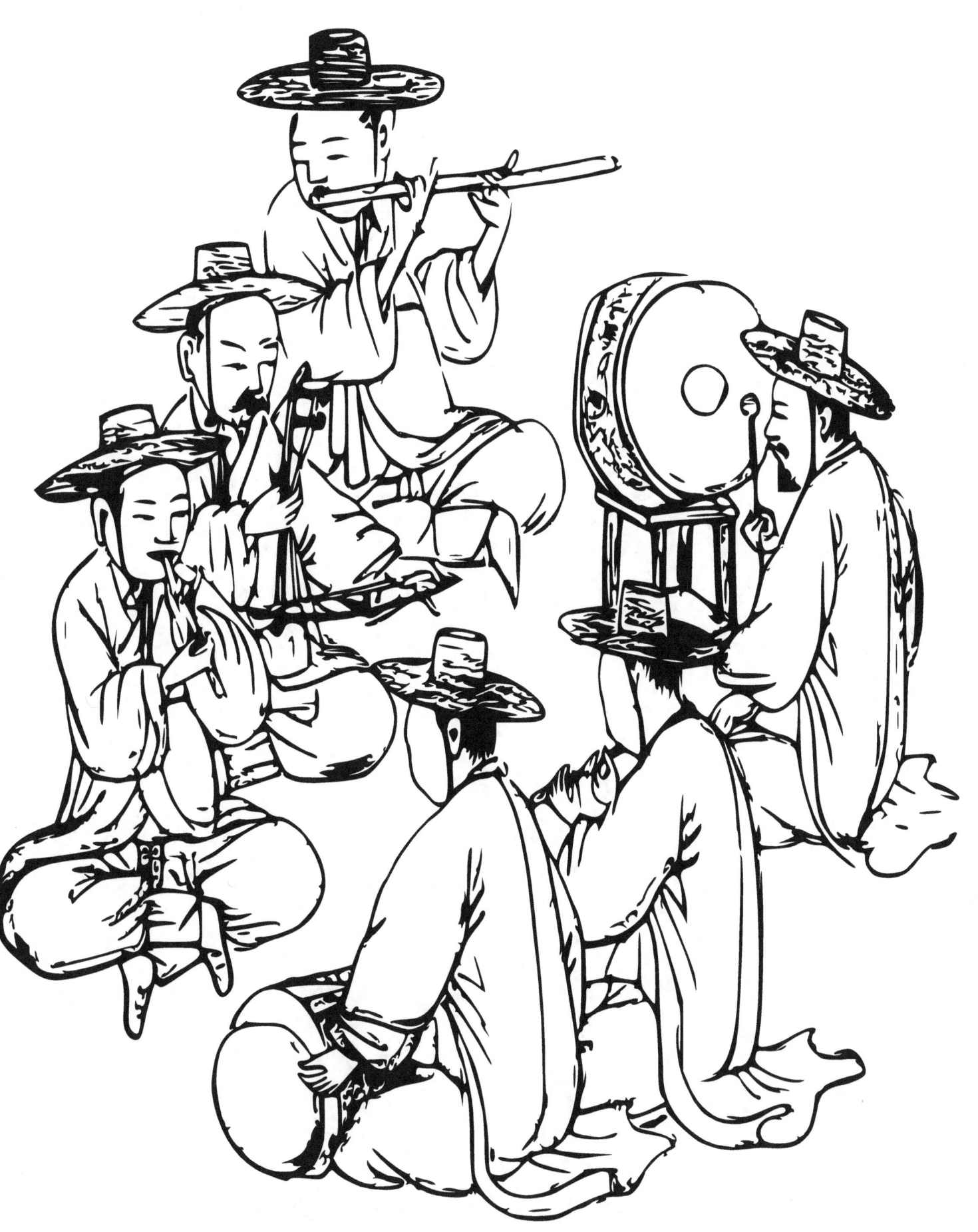

ALL RIGHTS RESERVED © 2020

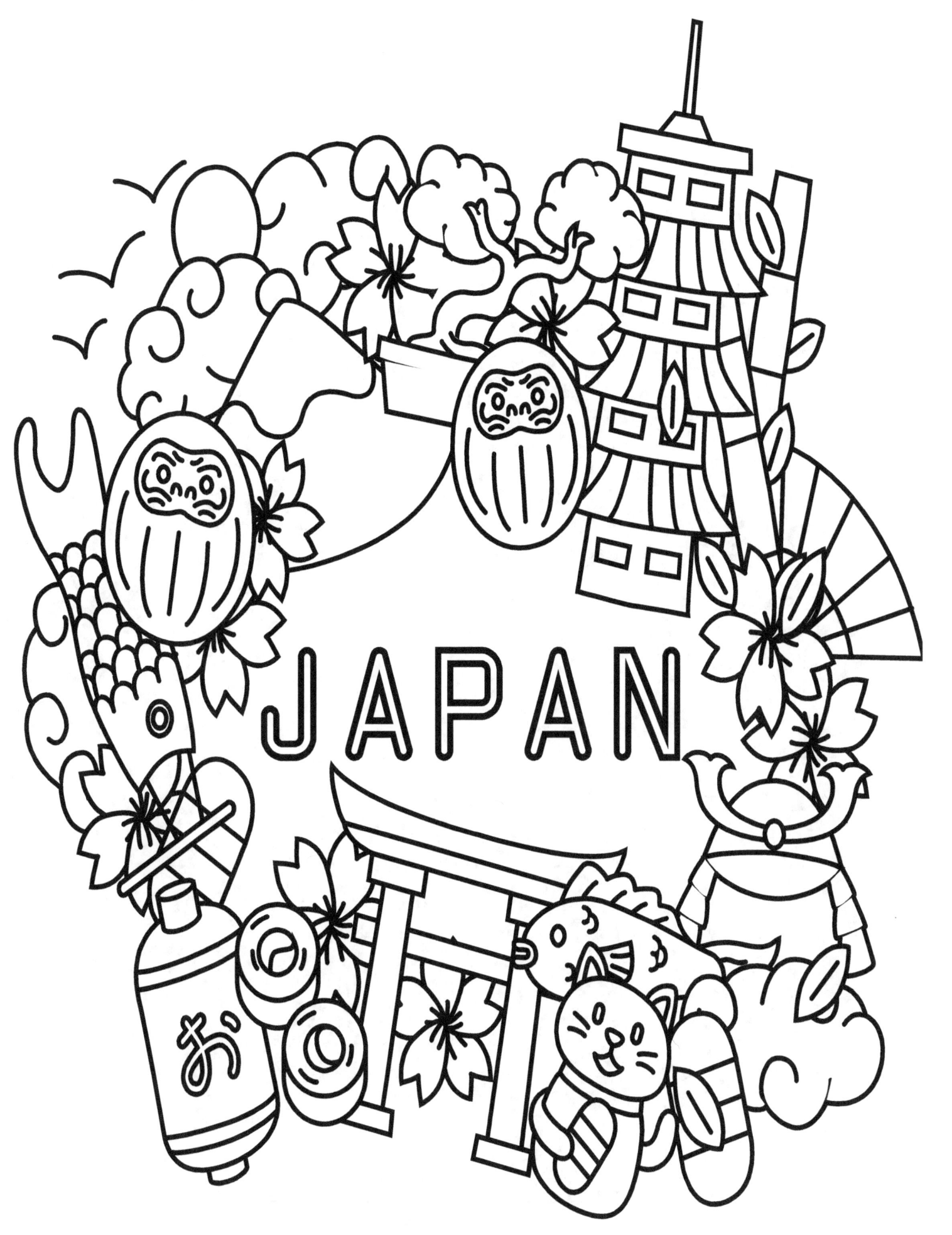

ALL RIGHTS RESERVED © 2020

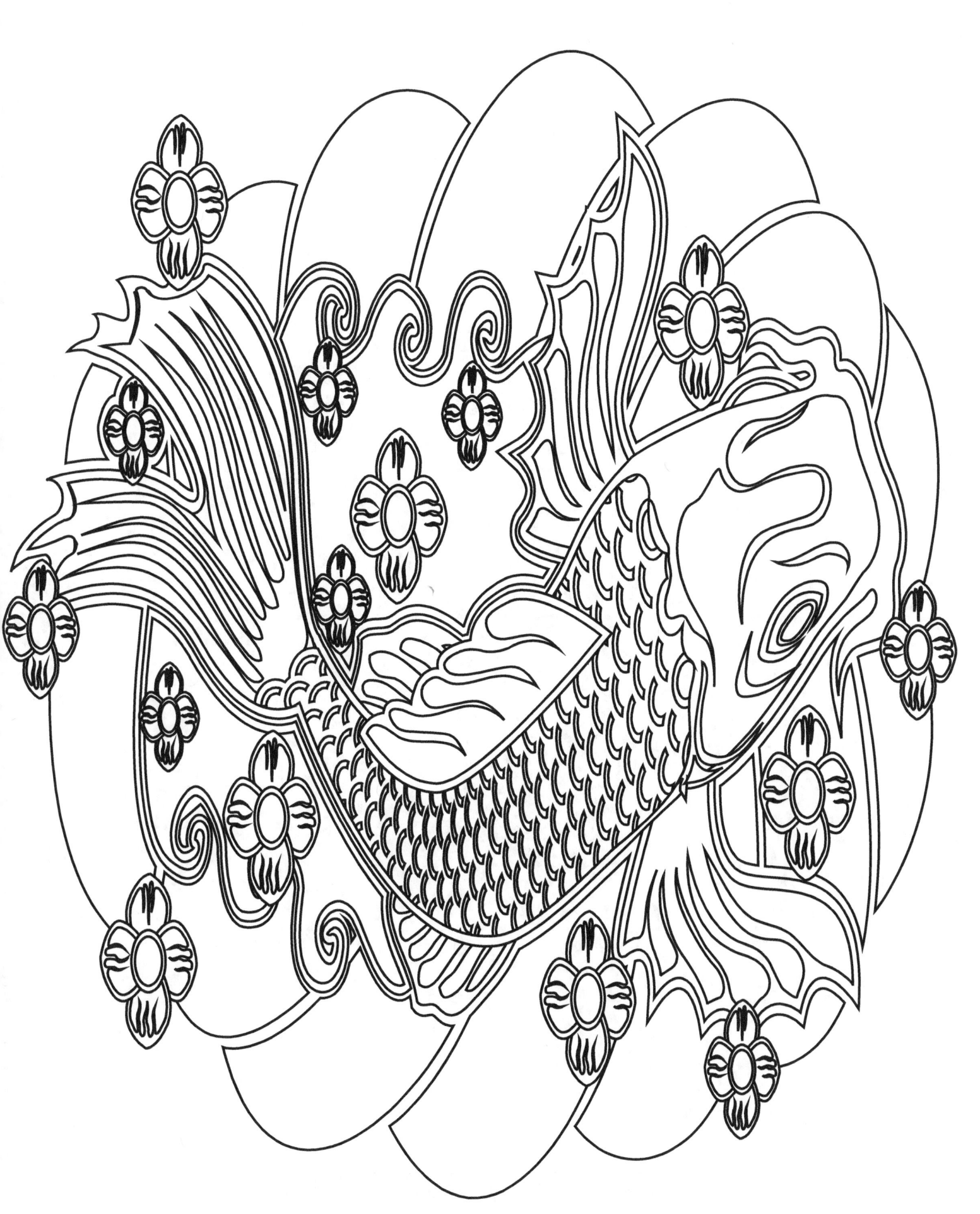

ALL RIGHTS RESERVED © 2020

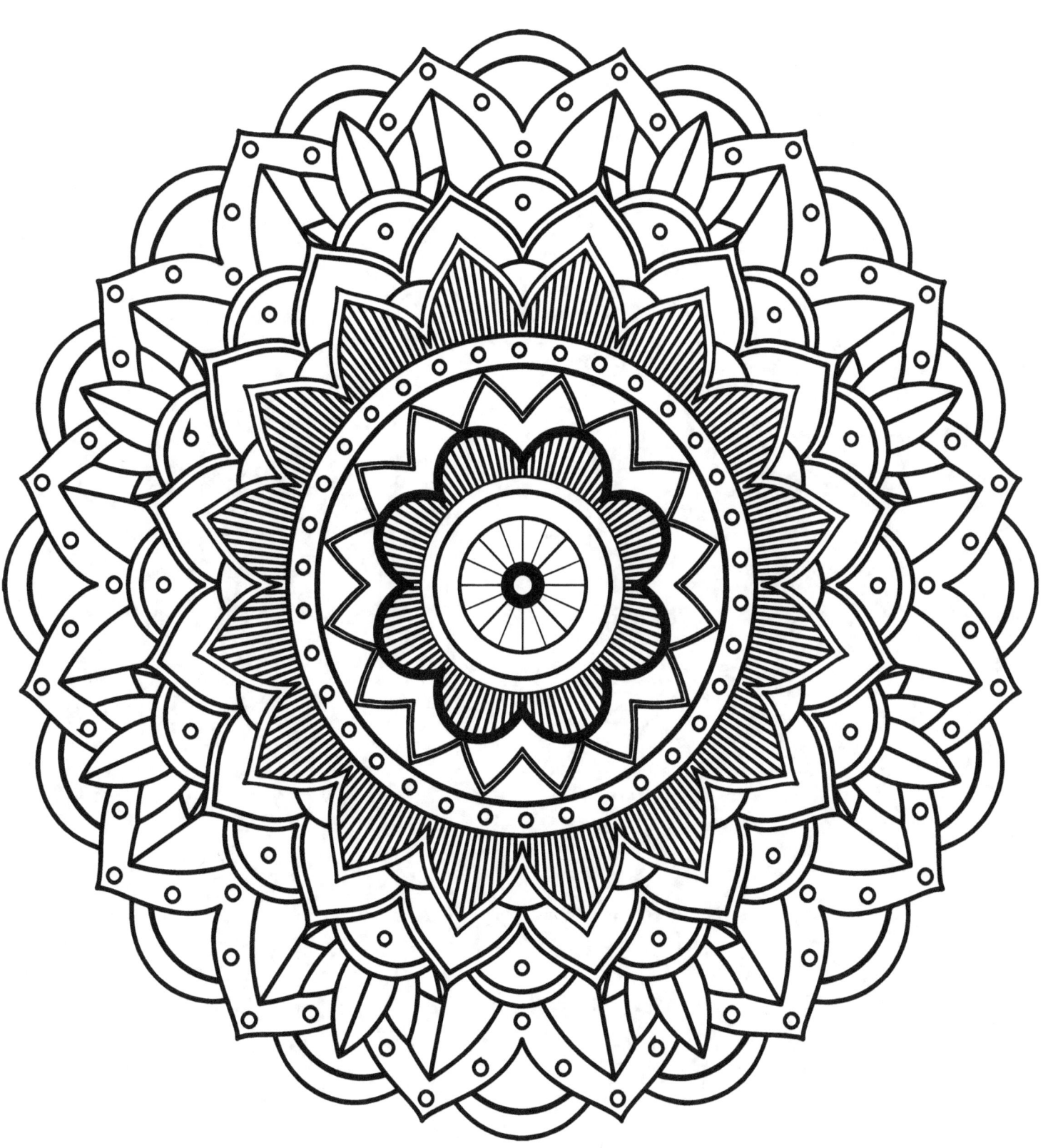

ALL RIGHTS RESERVED © 2020

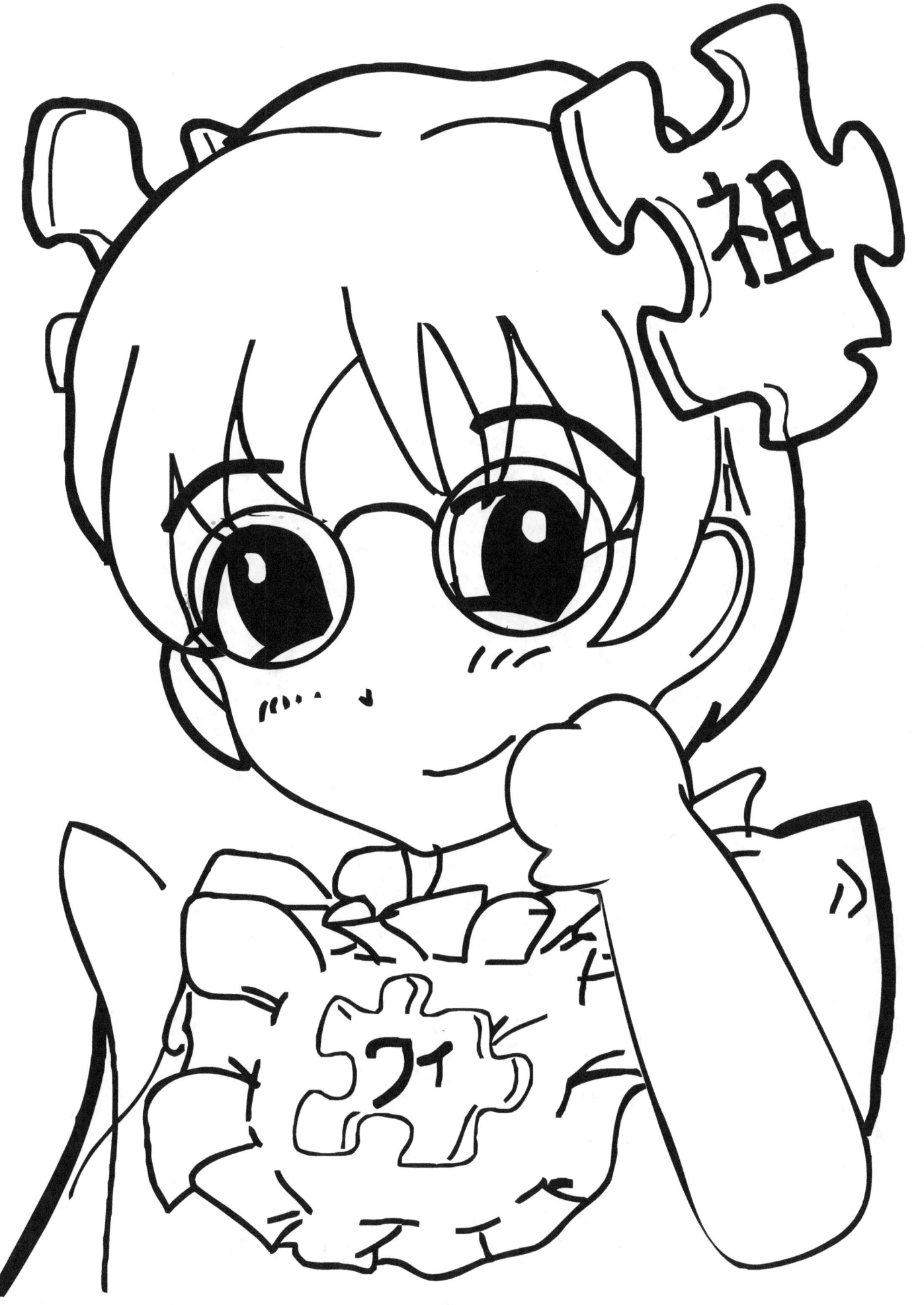

ALL RIGHTS RESERVED © 2020

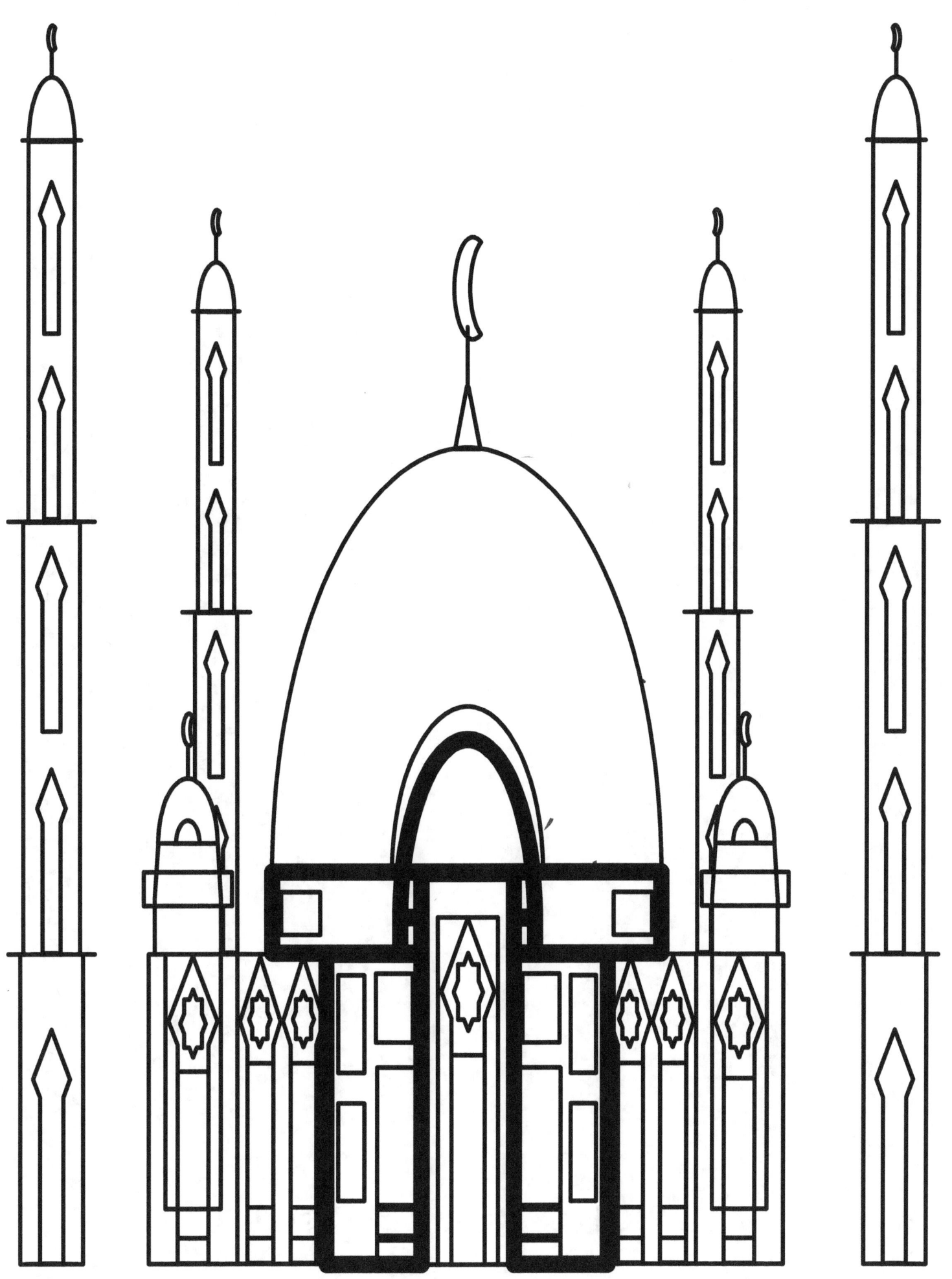

ALL RIGHTS RESERVED © 2020

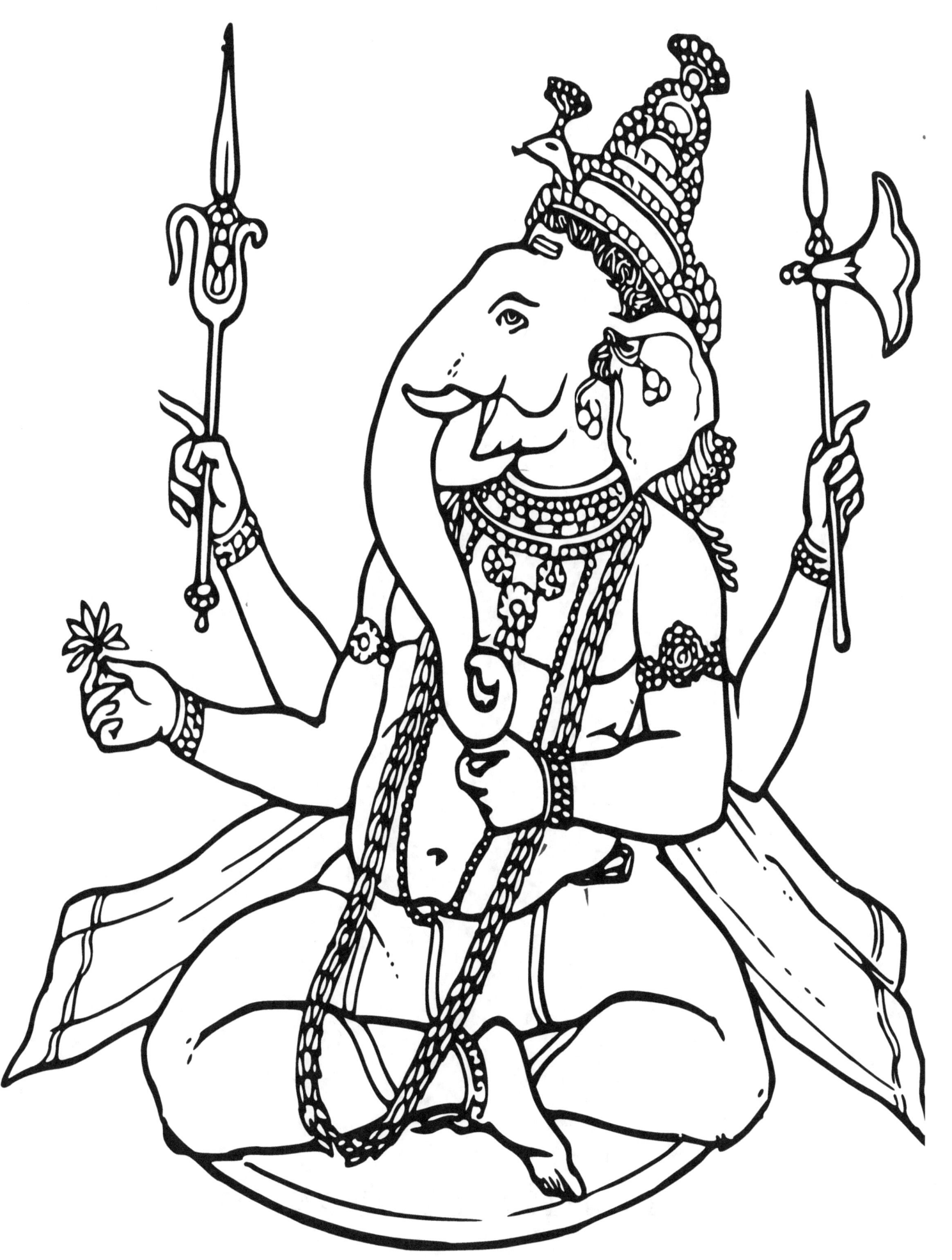

ALL RIGHTS RESERVED © 2020

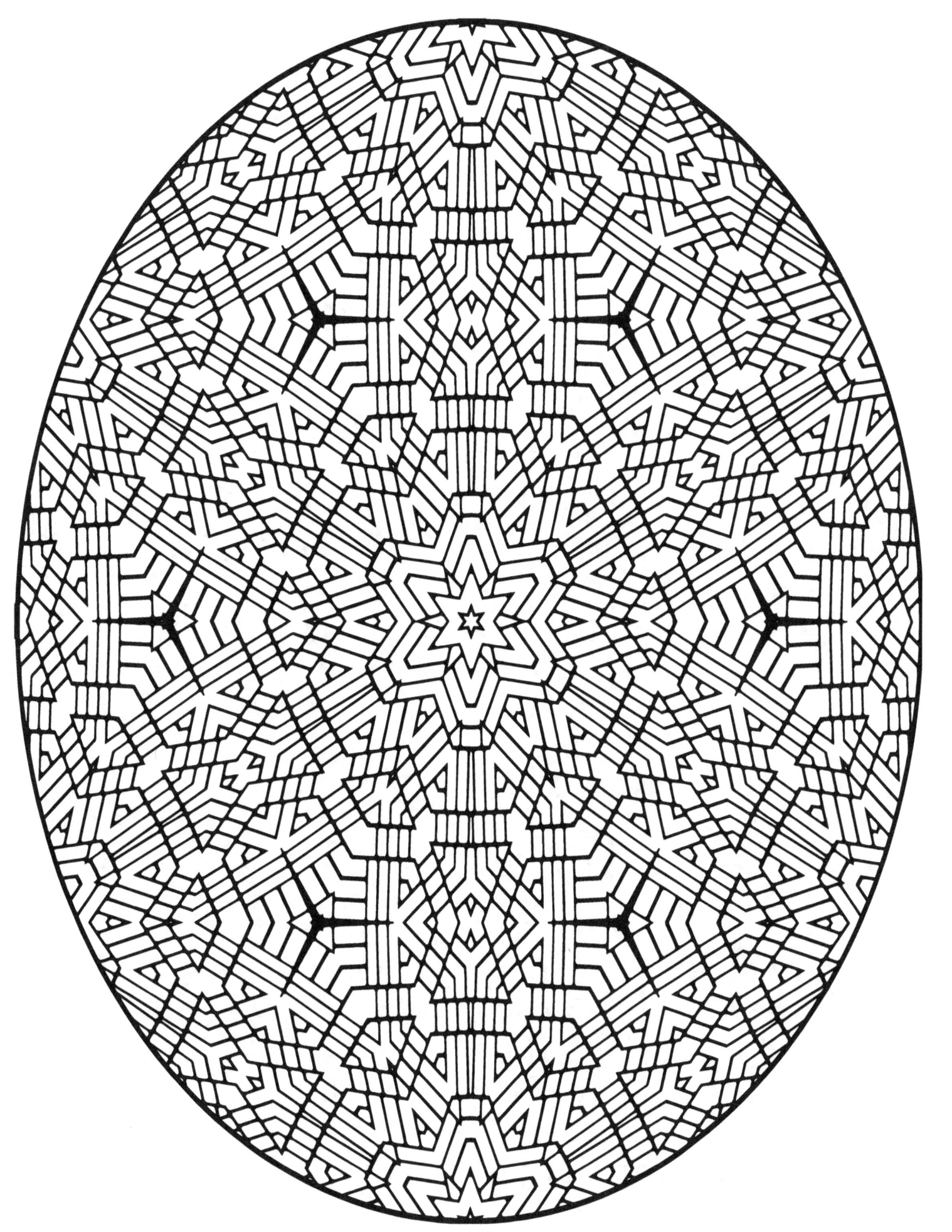

ALL RIGHTS RESERVED © 2020

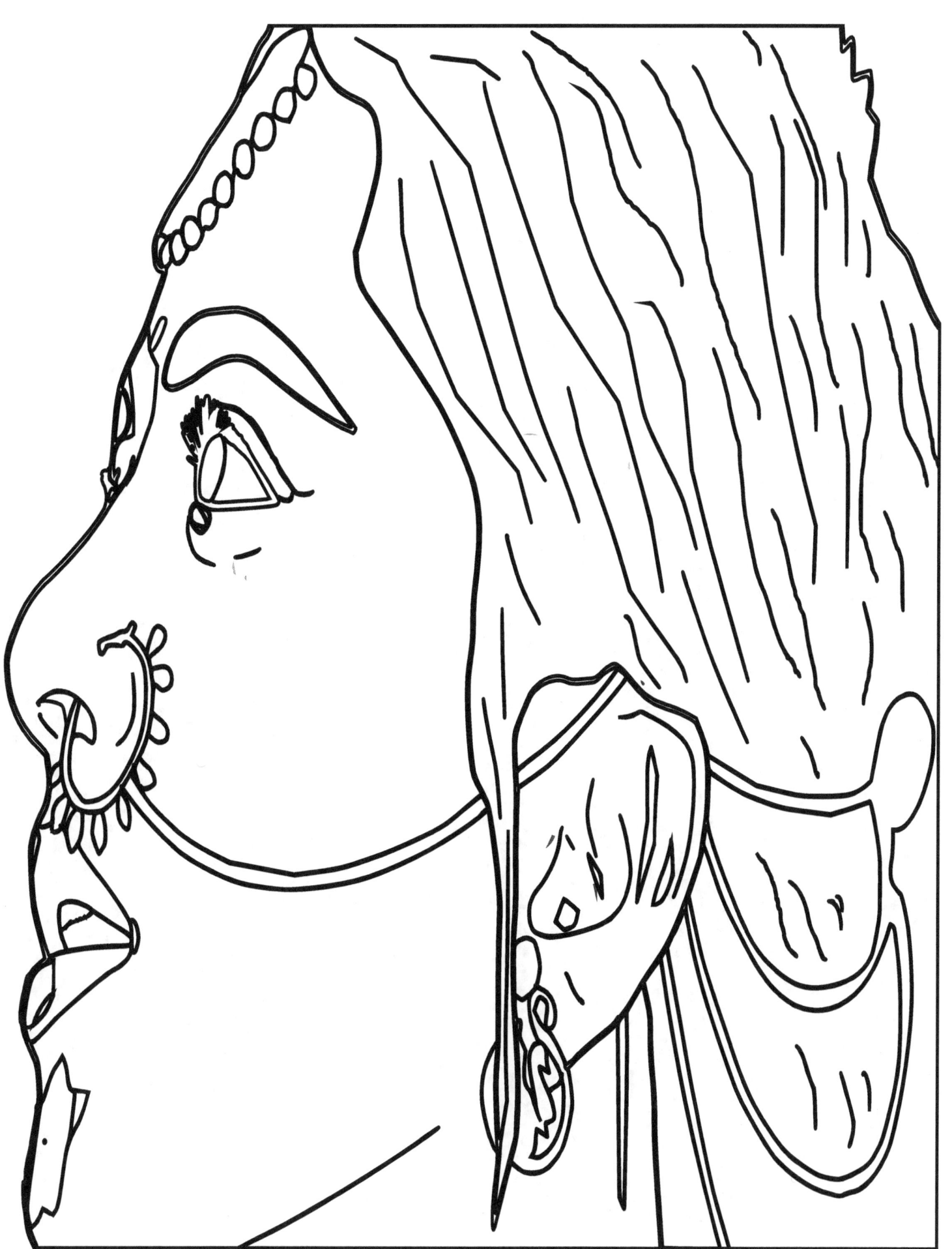

ALL RIGHTS RESERVED © 2020

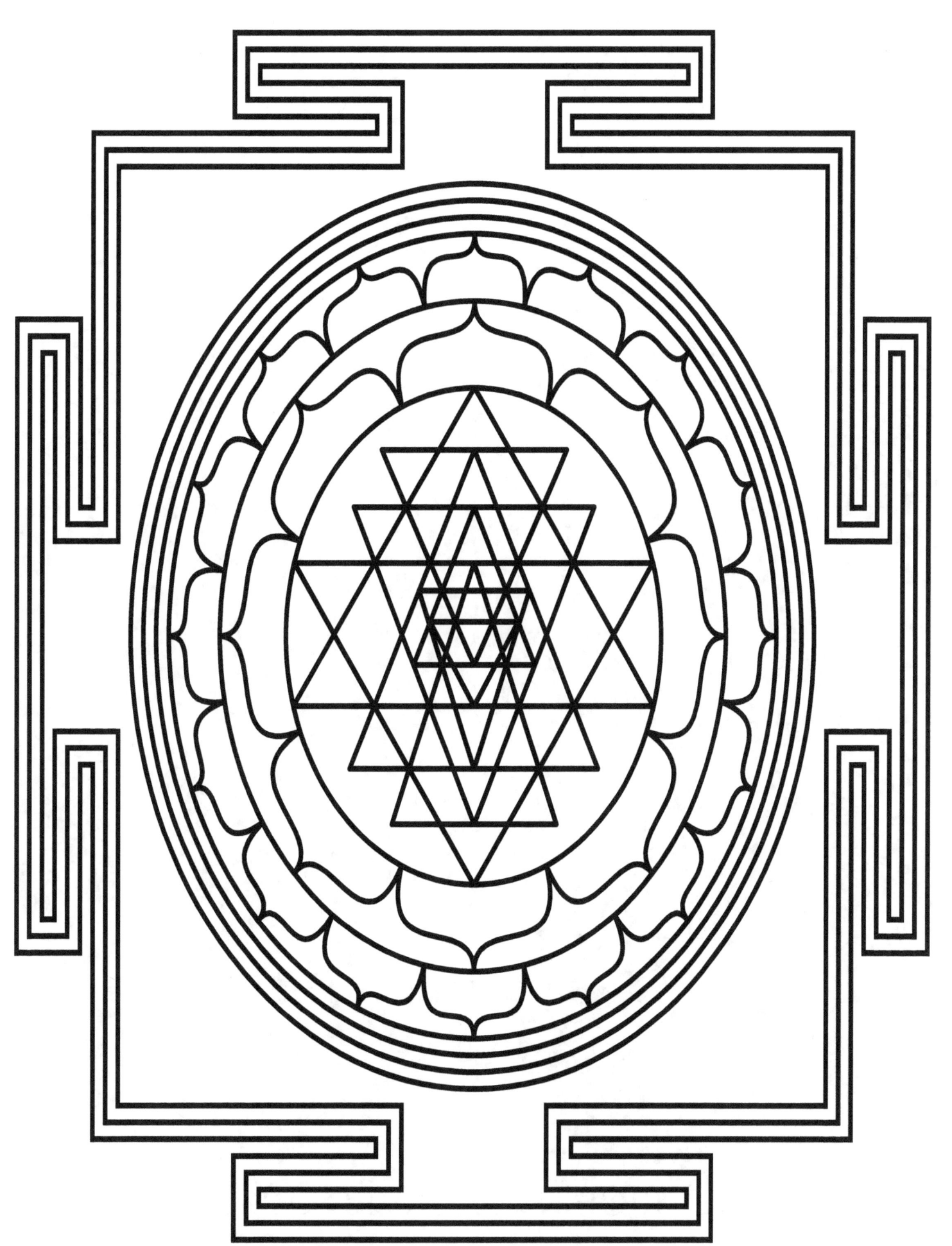

ALL RIGHTS RESERVED © 2020

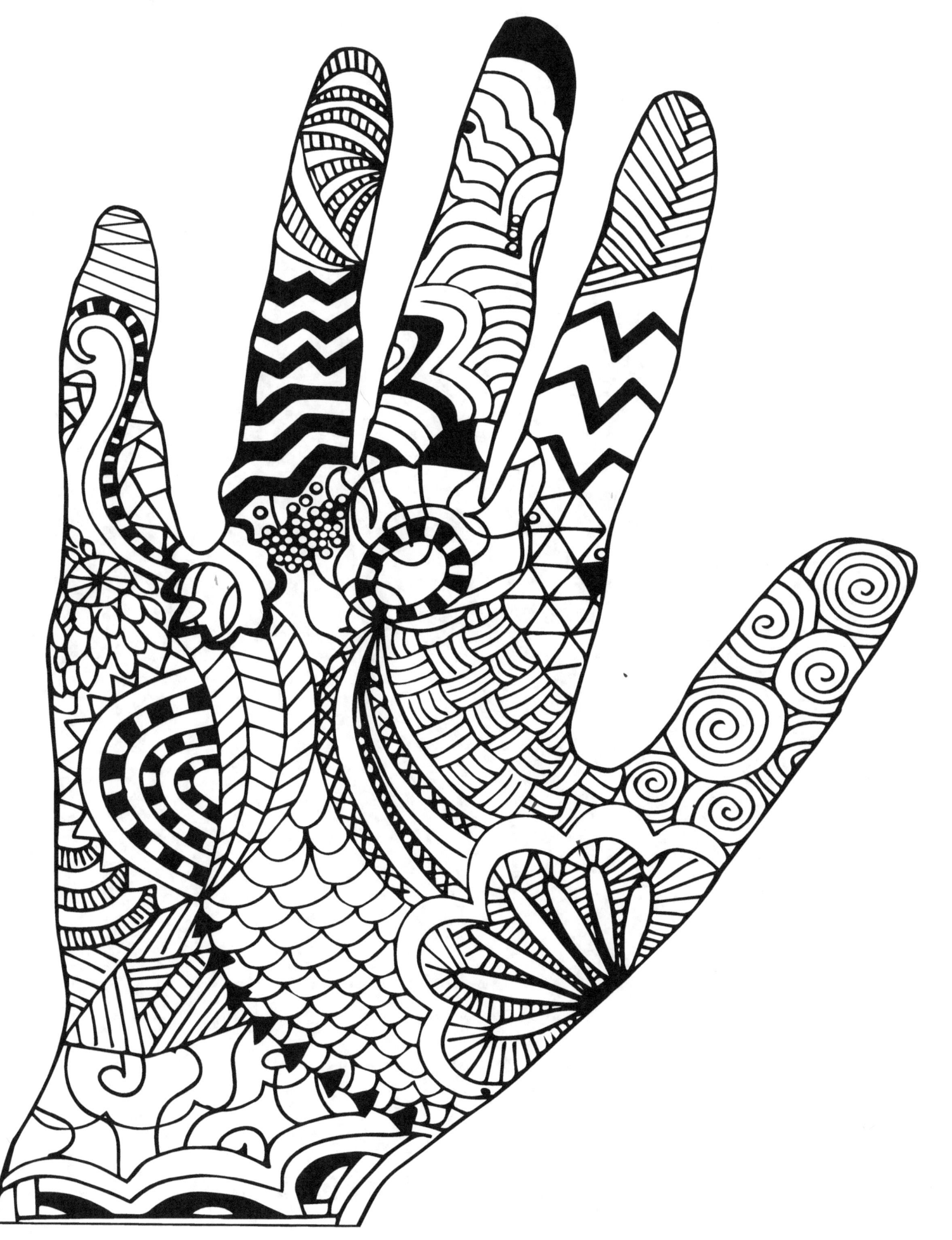

ALL RIGHTS RESERVED © 2020

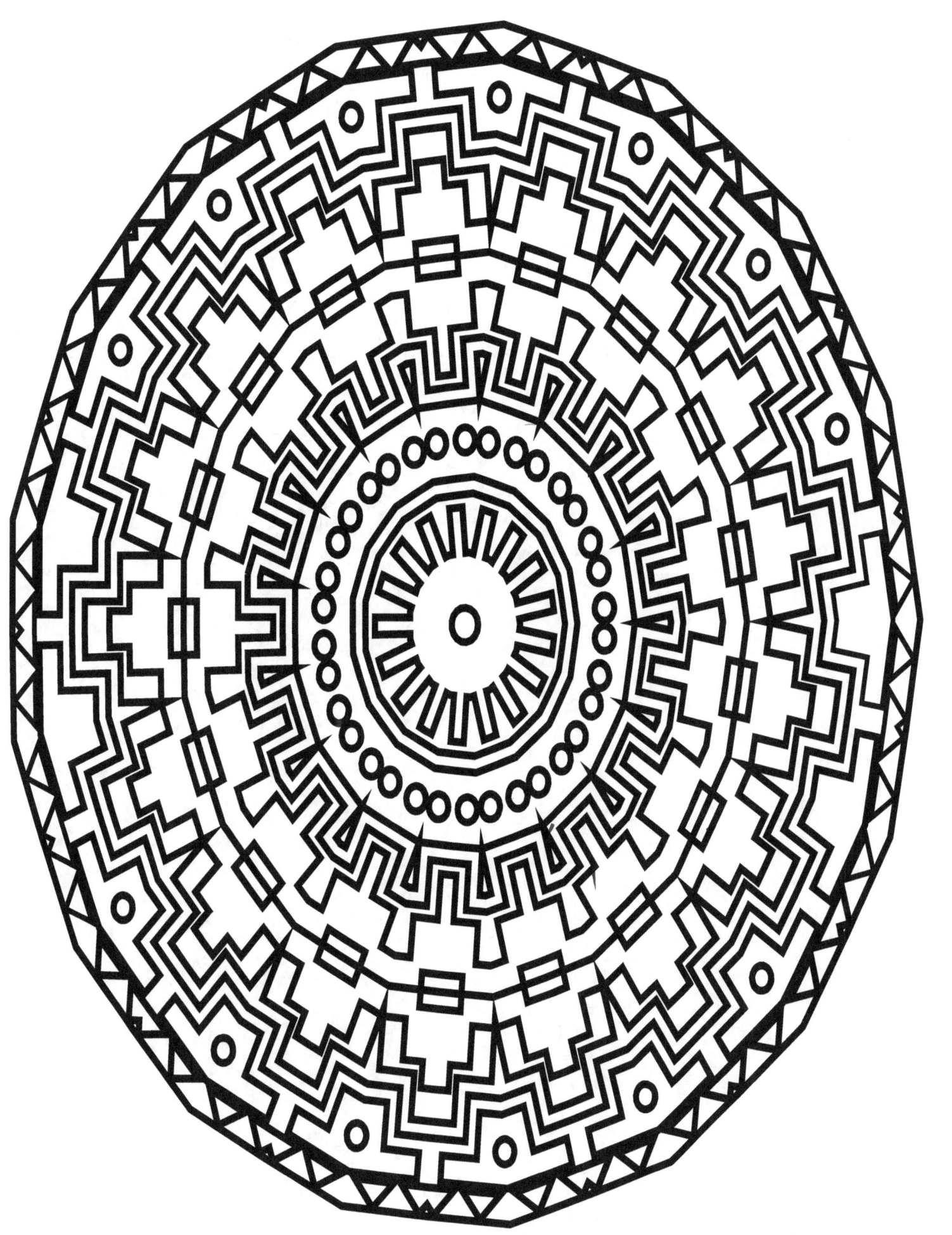

ALL RIGHTS RESERVED © 2020

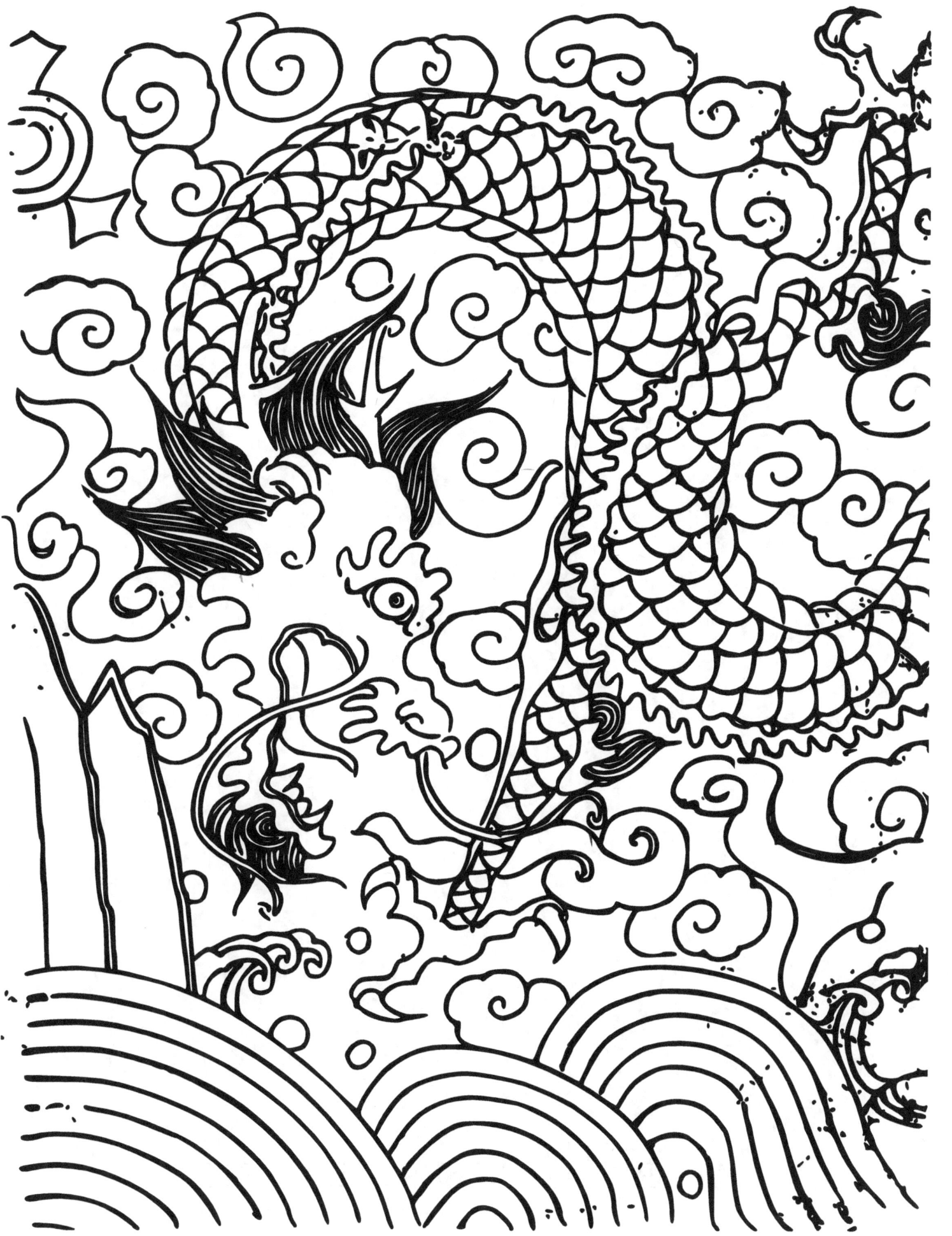

ALL RIGHTS RESERVED © 2020

www.ingramcontent.com/pod-product-compliance
Lightning Source LLC
Chambersburg PA
CBHW080952220526
45465CB00008BA/3260